WRITING
THE RIVER

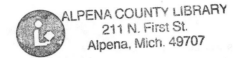
WRITING THE RIVER

POEMS
by
Luci Shaw

PIÑON PRESS

P.O. Box 35007, Colorado Springs, CO 80935

Library of Congress Catalog Card Number:
      94-10388
ISBN 08910-98232

Cover photo: David Caldwell
Author photo: John Shaw

Shaw, Luci.
      Writing the river / Luci Shaw.
          p. cm.
      ISBN 0-89109-823-2
      I. Title.
      PS3569.H384W75   1994
      811'.54—dc20   94-10388
                                                              CIP

Printed in the United States of America

WRITING THE RIVER

JOURNAL ENTRY, NOVEMBER 4, 1989

It has been raining hard for two days here in
Sudden Valley. We've had at least four inches.
The constant downpour has soaked the ground to
a sog, and the ground, in turn, has drained like a
full sponge into the creeks. My creek, Beaver
Creek, has risen from its customary low summer
profile of tea-dark water slow over pebbles (with
the stream shallow enough so that the pebble
tops poke, dry, above the surface) and has been
supercharged with the overflow from the rain.
All last night I heard it, my window open as usual
to let in the wet sounds and fragrances. Often I
could hardly tell in the dark if what I heard was
heavy rain, or rushing river water, or a liquid mix
of both.

This morning the rain has stopped, but the
stream is the color of cafe-latte—twelve turbulent
feet wide, and lapping at my house footings. The
whole course of the creek bed, the gash along the
bottom of this part of the valley, has changed.

It is never static. Sometimes, in August, it
almost stops, as if it is flowing cupful by cupful,
carefully conserving itself during the dry months.
But even that minimal movement is always fluid.

This creek is like my stream of consciousness.
All day and all night it is in the background of my
listening and thinking. It is there as I write, or
stoke the woodstove, or sleep (dreaming), or

make soup. I often peer out at it through the window, or step onto the deck to listen to it, as if I need to check it.

I think it is myself I am checking. Its flow is so like the flow of my own living or writing—slow, and reflectively lazy, sometimes, or full and fierce in the rush of ideas and work. It is my metaphor—intensely personal. I am writing a stream. I am living a creek. I either feel the pebbles grazing my stomach as I swim, or I half-drown in the torrent that follows the rain.

My other motif in this Sudden Valley life is the woodstove. Since I built this little house in the woods I have had to learn about the care and feeding of stoves. With its chunky black iron body (attached to the ceiling and out to the sky by a sort of periscope, the chimney stack) the stove is like a small child. It requires constant attention and nourishment if it is not to sulk and pant and go out on me, flames dying, embers cooling to a pile of nondescript ash and charcoal.

I attend to this phenomenon out of necessity rather than esthetics, but with the same kind of mythic consciousness as with the creek. Yes, I have electric baseboard heating, in obedience to the building code, but its outrageous expense drives me to the chopping of wood and the splitting of kindling—a messy, tedious, constant business, like writing. But like writing, it is warming, once it is lit and going enthusiastically, to both body and soul.

WRITING THE RIVER

After two day's rain heavy enough to
circle the view with descending silver
Beaver Creek has grown to the size of

a metaphor—rising fast from summer,
slow over pebbles, to this rowdy
torrent. Under my window it hurls itself,

with the force of myth, over river stones,
down rapids, riddled with fish.
All day the voice of water roars

behind my writing—all day, while I'm
making soup, stoking the woodstove
(the flames rushing their orange rivers

up the chimney). Under a darkening sky
I step out on the porch to check its
scouring race, and is it rising still? It is

myself I am checking, keeping the window
open all night to that naked
splendid sound, dark as pewter. Rainfall

and river together—rinsing the room,
soaking my dreams. In one dream
I am a salmon working my way up

the valley, grazed by rocks. I am living
a creek, writing a river. Downstream,
a trace of my blood feeds the Sound.

Luci Shaw

To my sons, John & Jeff

*The author wishes to give grateful acknowledgment
to the editors of the following periodicals
in which some of these poems first appeared:*

Burning Light, The Christian Century, Crux,
First Things, Image, Kinesis, Leadership Journal,
Perspectives, Radix, The Rolling Coulter, South
Coast Poetry Journal, The Sow's Ear, Studio

*Eight poems in this volume were included in a Festschrift
in honor of Dr. James Houston
of Regent College, Vancouver*

*Three poems in this volume were chosen for the anthology
Odd Angles of Heaven,
David Craig and Janet McCann, Editors*

CONTENTS

I Diamonds that leap

II A bird in the church

III Writing the river

I

DIAMONDS THAT LEAP

SAILING: SAN FRANCISCO BAY

She braces — one hand
on the forestay. Her other hand
curves around to the outside
of the jib, its belly heavy with wind.

Pressing against her hand-heel,
deceptive as silk, the air
fills the sail cloth until it bulks
as pregnant as her own body
before the last birth. Out there
on the Catalina's prow, with
the small waves swelling against
the hull under her so that
through the soles of her deck shoes
she feels the waters breaking,
she is alone, letting it all go
with the water sliding away below.
The other sounds — curlew cries, Mozart
on the portable player, the glasses
and voices from the cabin — trail
behind, like the faint calls of her
grown children, gone in the green wake.

It is all such old magic — bittersweet
like birth, the melting sea silver
stained sky red, vanishing between
her legs like the last light being sucked
down through the bones of the mountains,

there, in a bloody show.
She flattens her hand and pushes hard
against the blue cloth so that the sail
spills some of its wind,
giving it back to the bay.

AT THE CLOISTERS

On the stone wall, in shadow,
Madonna and Child, with the Child
gone. Bearing the baby
she'd lately borne — cradling him
who upholds the whole world —
stands Mary, fractured by
an unbearable gravity not
her own. It must be that pull,
and the violence of time,
which has broken her hands off
at the wrists.

Through blank air, past
the small, missing face,
she catches my eye. We exchange
a wry secret: our common breakage
mends the gap of years as we both
let our children go, and learn
the start of weight loss —
its holy levity. Oh!

LABOR

After her daughter's wedding
she cleaned out the bedroom — rolling up
the posters of Venice, the Greek
Islands, virginal sails like wings
in golden bays. Surveying the naked
closet and walls from the doorway
she felt the chill, as though
she had just expelled
her afterbirth. And from

some deep place she remembered —
that beginning of loss, a pushing out
and out that left the matrix hollow.
The newborn's muted cry still
echoes — another expulsion,
another wave goodbye.
Every division of cells widens
the change; the ripples circle out;
the boat leaves harbor.

SUNDAY AFTERNOON
AT THE NURSING HOME

As green peas swell, they shape and split
their pods. On the cold linoleum
under the bed her slippers lie, slight
as a child's. For a decade her small-boned feet
have molded them, like discarded seed cases.
Long ago her genes were sown into our soil.
(I have her shrug, her small ears;
my brother has the vitality and verve
her body has surrendered.) Now
she is shrunk all over, arthritis
curling her hands like dried leaves.

The curtains, with the same generic
blossom pattern as all the other rooms along
the hall, are always drawn; after cataracts
she shuns the glare of the world (gardens
blaze unseen outside). Her geraniums,
in pots along the sill, are dying
for lack of light, their petals blood-dark.
The only colors in the room
bloom in the family snapshots we try to send
often: from one wall the party dresses
of her four great-granddaughters unfold, bright
as flowers—iris, poppy, periwinkle, marigold.

WHEN YOUR LAST PARENT DIES

Move up to the top of the ladder.
Looking down over your shoulder you can see
the replicas from your own body crowding the rungs
all the way down. Precarious, you teeter there

on the final step with nothing for your hands
to hold. They grab at emptiness. The glancing
stars are falling around you. Cosmic dust
stings your eyes. There is no one above you

to compass the wideness of space. You
are the final clasp that buckles
earth to heaven. Somehow, you
must hold up the ladder, heavy with life.

ST. FRIDESWIDE'S CHAPEL

CHRIST CHURCH CATHEDRAL, OXFORD

In this ancient place
one section of the fresco
ceiling has been left
to peel, a puzzle, half
the pieces lost. As from
the bottom of a well I stare
up, waiting for revelation.
A raw plaster frowns
from the past, a closed sky, murky
as thunder, traced with

gold shreds—a snatch
of hair, a broken chin line,
wing fragments in red, in blue.
My eyes are busy—deepening
pigment, filling in the detail
of hands, feathers, touching up
the face of an angel. But nothing
changes. The terrible inscrutability
endures, deeper than
groined arches. Tattered

seraphim flash their diminishing
edges, like the chiaroscuro God who,
if we believe Michelangelo, touched
Adam into being with one finger,
whose footprints crease the blackness
of Genesaret, whose wing feathers

brush our vaulted heaven, purple
with storm, whose moon
is smudged—a round, glass window,
an eye moving between clouds.

THE OVERSHADOW

". . . the power of the Most High will overshadow you . . ."
LUKE 1:35

When we think of God, and
angels, and the Angel,
we suppose ineffable light.

So there is surprise in the air
when we see him bring to Mary,
in her lit room, a gift of darkness.

What is happening under that
huge wing of shade? In that mystery
what in-breaking wildness fills her?

She is astonished and afraid; even in
that secret twilight she bends her head,
hiding her face behind the curtain

of her hair; she knows that
the rest of her life will mirror
this blaze, this sudden midnight.

MOVING

In the closet, one broom waits. Two
plates. A mug for my final thirst.
A light bulb to see by, but
the bookcases are blank boxes
of air. Dents in the gray rug
mark the long-time places of
occasional chairs, left askew now
in the new, smaller space on the eleventh
floor, six miles away.
In that narrow hall
the cartons are piled, marked "tools,"
"Christmas ornaments," "blue/white
china."

Last night, in the room where
my husband died,
I slept for the last time.

Or didn't sleep, my heart
leaping unpredictably, like a fish
from a lake.

NAIL

Like the two-inch spike
you drove into the inside
of the closet door,
remembering hangs
on a tenuous hiddenness.
When the door closes
the nail is gone, all
but my instinct about where to go
to hang the blue cotton pajamas
when, in early light,
I slip them off.

EVAPORATION

Twenty years ago the green square beyond
our back door was webbed with lines
on which I hung with wooden pegs
my angels and my ghosts — white nightgowns
winged in the wind, shrouds of tablecloths,
shirts fluting their spooky sleeves, their
dwindling tails — shadows of the lucid cloth
moving like water on the grass.

Now we live over a basement dryer churning
beneath a 40-watt bulb. The trap keeps filling
with a gray lint as my clothes, my second skins,
are dried out by the minute, on a dial.
The air behind the house
is empty of epiphanies, apparitions.
Gone is the iron-fresh smell of damp linens
praying their vapor to the sun.

VIRGIN

As if until that moment
nothing real
had happened since Creation

As if outside the world were empty
so that she and he were all
there was—he mover, she moved upon

As if her submission were the most
dynamic of all works; as if
no one had ever said Yes like that

As if one day the sun had no place
in all the universe to pour its gold
but her small room

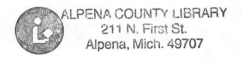

TRACE

Because you walk
on water
your footprints
are invisible

We look in vain
for a wet mark
from the ball
of your foot
or even
a lick of
dried salt
on the stones

STIGMATA

The tree, a beech, casts the
melancholy of shadow across the road.
It seems to bear the enormous weight of
the sky on the tips of its branches.
The smooth trunk invites me to finger

five bruise-dark holes where rot
was cut away. Years
have pursed the thickened skin
around the scars into mouths
that sigh, "Wounded. Wounded."

As the hurt feels me out
wind possesses the tree and
overhead a hush comes; not that
all other sounds die, but half a million
beech leaves rub together in the air,

washing out bird calls, footsteps,
filling my ears with old pain,
and a song of cells in sun.
"Hush," they say
with their green lips. "Hush."

CROSS

On my chest this Friday afternoon,
the elegant small signature
of violent death
swings as I walk, gold tapping my
deep heart, telling me I was there.
*(I did not mean to do it; I did
not know.)* I slump under the weight
of it; my pulse
echoes the beat of hammers.

A POET'S CALENDAR

Like a rosary by which I tell
the blessings of night and day —
their dark, credal hymns and radiant
mysteries — the moon in its phases,
white on dark blue, arcs across
the month. Its discs, like
vertebral cushions, space out
my spine of time
to mind me of flexion, reflection.

Sometimes a life seems like
one long month of years,
every completed day slipping away
behind, a bead on a string.
Voicing crescent words in silver,
or growing pregnant with vowels
round as pearls, I lean lopsided,
like a moon, towards
my lunatic perfection.

DIAMONDS THAT LEAP

When the leaf fell and brushed my hand
I began to reverse the world. I asked:
What if this warped willow leaf, yellow,

scaled with age, could smooth
to a green blade and flicker into
the knot of a spring twig, like

a grass snake's tail disappearing, slick
and chill, into his home? That one question —
it was a whirlpool, pulling in

others: What about a river?
Might its waters rush up these indigo
hills of Shenandoah and split to a scatter

of diamonds that leap to their rain
clouds, homing? Can a love
shrink back and back to like,

and the crack of a small, investigative
smile? Could God ever suck away creation
into his mouth, like a word regretted,

and start us over?

Harrisonburg, Virginia, Fall 1990

II

A BIRD IN THE CHURCH

MAJOR THEME TO A MINOR TUNE

The sky is black as an empty heart.
The sky is pierced with stars loud as angels,
And all I can exclaim to myself is *Mirabile!*
This is a time of premonition, and sharp surprise,
and scurrying feet.

From the eaves icicles fall and break with
the tinkle of bells.
In the wind dead leaves scatter, spent as straw in
a dull manger.
All I can mutter is *Amen!*
This is a month of frosts, and rebuff,
and questions hard as birth.

Astonishment—as a baby bursts bloody from
the womb.
Air spins from his fresh lungs like a word
so that all we can chant—a mass in A minor—
is *Kyrie:*
This is a season of serial visions, and a bodily God,
and a sword in the heart.

GHOSTLY

I think often about the invisible
God—doubly covert. I mean, now and again
Father and Son made their appearances,
speaking bold in thunder, blood,
or salvation. But the third
Person is a ghost. Sometimes
he silvers for a moment, a moon sliver
between moving leaves. We aren't sure.

What to make of this . . . How
to see breath? As energy
hovering, birdlike, over chaos,
breeding it into ferns and whales;
blessing the scalps of the righteous
with a pungency of oil; bleeding the hard
edge of warning into all those
prophet voices; etching
Ezekiel's view with oddities—
eyes in wheels spinning like astrolabes;
crowding Mary's womb to seed its
dark clay; wising up fools to improbable
truth; filling us like wine bottles;
bursting from our mouths in champagne gasps
of surprise? This for sure—he finds
enough masks to keep us guessing:
Is it really you? Is this you also?

It's a cracked, crossover world, waiting
for bridges. He escapes our categories,
choosing his shapes—fire, dove,
wind, water, oil—closing the breach
in figures that flicker within
the closed eye, tongue the brain, sting
and tutor the soul. Once incarnate
in Judaea, now he is present
(in us in the present
tense), occupying our bodies—
shapes to be reshaped—
houses for this holy ghost. In our special
flesh he thrives into something
too frequent to deny, too real to see.

PERFECT CHRISTMAS TREE

Jesus Evergreen, from top to toe
your springy boughs are hung
with surprise—a gift here, a gift
there—wreathed with a glitter
of graces, all your needles
lacy with air and the remembrance
of small snow, your freshness
filling the house with the festal
smell of the forest. Your tough
length has bent to the wind, the axe,
but now the centering trunk
lances straight up, piercing
your slow green dying with the ache
of being felled. While the rooted
mountain spruces sing, resin
bleeds from your cut heart.

SPARROW FALLING

A shifting net of birds swelling
over the pasture, turning, an amoeba,
now dark and granular as dying, now
an invisible, a thin fluid slicing light.

Folding, the winged black flock splits.
Plunges. My heart tumbles in the dark, and
against the backlit sky I am a bird—one of
a crew of sparrows, a weightless ha'pennysworth.

We fly bunched, then abruptly string ourselves
parallel on threads of phone wires,
a thousand voices humming through
our beads of claws. And off again.

My retina crowds with flight patterns
inking the hollow where wind has sucked
away, leaving the sky a great
stillness. God. These are not

words of birds. Some cries are black
beyond language. I feel, clotting
on my tongue like a shadow feather, a sparrow
is falling. A sparrow is falling.

—On the death of a friend's husband

A BIRD IN THE CHURCH

The black bird, not caught like us at
one lowly level, has entered this
stone cage of a church
with its fluidities of enclosed light.

Between crossbeam and cornice, wide
and high and low and up again, through
the sun's transfixing shafts, her wings
open and close in a bewilderment

of interior air, until, homing,
she glides down the path of light
behind the altar, and settles
high on the arm of the crucifix.

Having found a nesting tree,
she lodges at last where vertex
and horizon meet, resting in
the steady pain of Christ's left eye.

Oxford, July 1991

LIGHT GOES TO THESE
GREAT LENGTHS

Early. The alders begin to be backlit.
I'm sorry, but it is not enough.
How can I stay curled in shadow
until sunrise? Waiting is always

longer than the time it takes.
The mystery of slow light
has a power to awaken small birds.
Flighty juncos begin

to cut the gray silk of the air
and mend it behind them;
their darting
joins twigs to feeder-tray.

Now, *here*, a point of light strikes
through mist like a match, kindling
the loose leaves already
singed with color. Light goes

to these great lengths. A vapor rises
like smoke; again the perennial,
flameless humus burn begins. A feather
drifts down like a lost wing.

AT THE ORATORY, EDGBASTON
MAY 5, 1991

Ranks of suns, stars, moons dance with angels
on the cerulean ceiling. From outside,
under the real sun, a coterie of doves
calls in to the choir of boys —
a repeating antiphon cool and round as
the arched openings.

                    Gerard, this is where
you came to climb higher into God. Visitors
at mass a century later, we sit at the back.
Warmed, this chilled spring day, by remnants
of your ardor, we listen ourselves into the liturgy
that swells around us.

                    With the Kyrie
incense rises in slow clouds from censers;
its specks climb the slope of light like
a scale, raised by praise. And down
that same stair creeps gold, a compassionate
flush of it, the stained glass printing
its hot colors on the cold stone transept
like love come down so far
to find our level, to pool along the hearts'
floor, to burn there, on the spot where
you, too, received it, and were received.

*The poet G. M. Hopkins was received into
the Catholic Church October 21, 1866,
at the Oratory, Edgbaston.*

ONE OF TWELVE

FOR LINDA PASTAN

Had God singled out
one of Adam's other ribs
our first mother might
have been impeccable, turning
from the serpent's kiss,
spurning the seething fruit,
walking naked with the man,
wanton with light.
Even you, even I might have been
born whole enough to swim, without
drowning, the river of
God's will, a race swift as Tigris,
a gold warm as Euphrates.

Imagine a country without
walls or gates, evergreen,
every frond glossy with spring.
Vision our vile bodies preserved
for bliss, not lust, not dying.
Conceive of peace,
a pearl shining at the world's heart.
(Yes. And perfection tugs, still,
like heaven, at every cell.)

Eve, though, was the chosen bone
(in which our own dry skeletons
lay layered, waiting for breath),
one of twelve, like Reuben who went

up to his mother's bed, or Judas
grabbing his bloody silver,
or January, this darkest
of a year of months. Yet
January's chill—which is, like
pride, the death of gardens—harks back
by a dozen days to the primal Sowing,
the Advent Seed dug in to die, sprouting
its improbable winter green shoot
for which I wait—a garden, not in Eden
but in me—Epiphany, unflawed fruit
of the twelve days of Christmas.

THREE HAIKU: QUEEN ANNE'S LACE

It lifts its lovely,
loose exactness—like fireworks,
outstarrings of God.

Cut, it rebels at
the constriction of a vase,
foams into the dark.

Its small galaxy
traces a powder of stars
on the polished wood.

GREAT BLUE HERON

FOR NANCY IREMONGER

From the corner of
one eye I see an ungainliness
dropping its stilt legs past my window
onto the lily pond's edge. In
the fan of water that lifts
and lowers, lifts and lowers
across the grass, the wing feathers
fold from the shape of flight
into a blue umbrella—almost purple
against the green.

To sight a heron is
a good omen, you told me once
after we had watched a
visitation. Like gray praying
prophets, heralds of something
Other, they elbowed their way
down to the creek that
threads itself around my wild
cabin, north of here by at least
a thousand miles.

What does it mean to see
an omen for good? Just this:
Because I love that far valley
of rain, I've wanted to believe
good. Now, in the haunting
of this holy stalker of water,

this picker of fish, its odd body
contoured wet in the sprinkler,
I follow a blue thread of promise
pulled south.

SPRING, ST. MARTIN'S CHAPEL, CATHEDRAL OF ST. JOHN THE DIVINE

FOR MADELEINE L'ENGLE

Both of us kneel, then wait
on the church chairs — square, chocolate brown —
knowing that soon the black priest

will hurry in, wearing his lateness like
the wrong robe. In the pregnant emptiness
before communion, that crack between worlds,

we listen inward, feet tight on the cold slate,
wanting to hear Christ tell us *Feed on me.*
Our hearts shiver, hidden. Nothing visible moves.

Outside a drizzle starts; drops spit on the sill.
The window bird flies motionless in
a cobalt sky of skillful glass.

But beyond the frame, plucking the eye
like a message from Outside, a minor shadow
tilts and swoops in light rain,

wings telling us to fly wide, loose
and nervy as pigeons who may peck crumbs from
any picnic table, or gnats right out of the air.

FINDING MYSELF

I am leaving a trail of
crumbs
broken off from my body
to feed friends, or the birds.
Or so I have always felt
as I shoulder the branches
aside and strike deep
into the woods
where grass overgrows
the old tracks.

Ahead of me now, on
the dark ground,
abruptly shines a white thing;
it wicks like
a lamp. And another.
I hear myself humming
an old song—a round—
as I stoop and finger
my own blaze of bread
turned hard as bone.

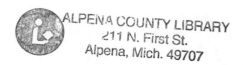

SKY LIGHTS

Moon and sun balancing at the
twilight's far ends. Eye of
silver following eye of gold.
Night and day dancing together in the sky.

I am a tale of opposites, morning/
evening, gold soul/silver spirit,
moon girl/sun woman alternating,
woven, and I cannot choose.

Night and day hold each other at arms'
length, eye to gleaming eye, a dialogue
of glances, and all the stars on the brink
of coming on like candles, or going out.

WHAT WE SAY WE WANT

What do we say when
that hunger harrows our bodies?

I love you. But it's not
that, or not only that.

Love is the word we use as an excuse
for all the pain, a white flag

dropped into the battle that rages
between urgency and fullness.

A time of exhaustion comes
when nothing is left to want;

or when what we still want
is too large to name.

CAMPING IN THE ROCKIES

After four days in the mountains
we have lived most of the world's
history—its passionate storms,
its silences of fog, the exuberant valleys
and ruinous cliffs, and above
the timber line its tundra of small,
pink flowers shivering on short wires,
that remind me of me, shivering
in the kiss of your breath.

Our uncertainty reveals itself
the way a mountain campanella
half-opens its purple mouth, waxy,
mysterious, tracked by a black thread
of ants. If I could be as sure about us
as the politicians seem to be about promises . . .
The truth is: the future lies
in ambush; more waits to happen

like the surprise of thunder,
when Glacier Lake, blue as a peacock
feather, carrying God's gold solar eye,
turns black with wind.

SNOWING: A TRIAD

I

Light holds its place
in a pond, frozen —
fixes a shadow in
the tangled woods —
even in the spaces between
the falling stars.

II

It is silver falling
like flour from a slow
sifter, filling up
the woods. In the whole
white world only the red sign
at the crossroads
is shocking enough to bring
us to a STOP.

III

Like a shroud wrapping
a dead body, snow
covers the small bushes,
the sallow grass. I'd like
to die like this, my roughness
smoothed, all
my old cracks filled.

EUCALYPTUS

The eucalyptus tree along the street
seems full of angels — the vertical
warps of leaves sloping like grey-green
wings penciled with early-morning light,
the breeze harping away
through the leathery feathers,
rattling the quite unheavenly
hanging strips of bark against the trunk.
The peeling of that tattered parchment,
scribbled with tree history, shows
the new skin, sleek as an egg — taut,
pearl, olive, apricot, glistening like silk —
though all the while a resin
bubbles out its darkening blood
from scratchings on the surface.
Just now the buoyant scent of eucalyptus oil
begins to lift the air to life
and stings into my nose the need
to breathe its healing in.

Its name starts out with good.
Eu — like the eucharist, and eulogy — good
gift of God, good word — and ends
with *kalypt* — covering; the frizzed cream flowers,
aging, cohere to form a cap that holds
the microscopic seeds within each woody nut.

From down below I see the gum-nut clusters—
each a "good hiding place" for secrets
too dark yet to be seen, or told.

Two years ago a ten-day freak,
a San Francisco freeze, blasted
the eucalypts and froze their juice
so even now, between the new festoons
of growth—greensilver shooting
fast enough to fill the sky with leaves—
a crispness rattles from the great,
dead branches, a leafy mutter that persists,
like the dry sound of my dead mother's voice
whispering her grievances at life,
at me, into my living ear.

From the bark-strewn path beneath,
I stare up into incongruity: sun
dapples the curling bark and satin skin.
And though the shadows lap across the trunk
like a blotched company of fallen spirits,
there's light enough to dazzle the massive bole;
to blaze between the angels' wings.

CARELESS FLYING

LUKE 12:24-26

I

I have been considering
the ravens, who live
without worrying
and have no bins or barns

and have no reaping machines.
Yet they are fed well—their bodies
sleek, gloved in black silk.
With what a minor tempest

they startle and settle,
yet they are the poets of motion.
Like folk songs their wings wheel
and hover, careless

as falcons. I am their
anxious scribe, listening myself
into their coarse
cries, storing the separate

notes in small black spaces
at the back of my skull.
God, if I were a bird I think
I would stop worrying.

Enough to wear, to eat. And one
more hour of life is, he says,
not worth the care. So, I'm
a bird. Nested in down,

I think I will float in a
dream of flight all night,
waking at the gold call of the sun
from the world's lip.

II
Francis, you could name me
your small sister.
You weren't a bird either
but you would know how to fold

your hands around my minor
warmth, then toss me, your arms
splayed, and let the air
catch me easy as feathers.

Watching ravens rise to God,
black steps moving on gold
ladders, gave you enough wonder
it took all your life

to revel in it. Your praise
escaped often to heaven, your eyes
following. Eventually you yourself
learned to fly, lifted by birds.

III

WRITING
THE RIVER

EDGES OF WALES

Stalking the blind lanes, striding to the hill
top before daybreak, often I've ached at the sweet chill
of spring light glittering through an intricacy
of leaves, when, in its precision of green, every tree
turns candle. With a series of airy, sharp surprises
crows's wings fold pearly heaven. Then the full sun rises,
polishing the view — stones quick and wet as steel,
glitter on a cobweb, gravel under my heel.

But on *this* early day in May, I wake
through light opaque as milk. The hedgerows make
mysteries with the mist. The cries of sheep shiver
the drenched air. Like silk sliding away, the river
moves south, the sheen of its crease
supple between banks and bushes blanched as fleece.
I thought I loved the hard, bright edges best
until I melted in this morning mist.

ON THE RIVER BANK, BIBURY

Why do you suddenly ask me am I happy?
I am only combing my mind, like water
searching the green weed. Under the plane
tree, in this confusion of suns, crescent

trout flip their golden spines
into the air, then straighten,
heads upstream, in the clear path of water.
I know now it is their bliss to be still

in a current. The fringed edges between glare
and dusk teach them how a river bank
casts a shadow of rest; how fixed and finite
lie the dark stones at river-bottom.

A POEM—ITS SELF-EXPOSURE

Sometimes, confessing, I incise
the skin over my breast-bone, between
my breasts, press the bone-saw's
intolerable teeth through
the knotting of sternum and ribs,
excavate the narrow valley floor
even deeper, open the vein of gold
that branches up from my mother lode,
unearth my molten heart for you, and
your dark, delicate, intrusive mining.

TRAVELING AT HOME

Often my living seems to condense
from sightings into words. I've trapped
most of my adventures on these dog-eared pages —
the frost-whiskered twigs, the crunch
of iced gravel under the tires, the snuff-
colored lenticular cloud resting like a cap
on the nearest peak, the sliding by
of steam risen from the river below,
its water mirror doubling the sky's indigo — all
are written down, plucked out of winter air,
fastened to a notebook sheet
by the black, pointed pin of ink.

Here: this is my life in my hands,
travelling the faint blue lines like back roads.
Though the landscapes are distant, the images
dance in my mind. Their primary colors.
Last January's morning in Montana reappears
and declares itself to me, like an old lover
to whom I was engaged once, proposing again.

BEACH AT ORIENT

FOR LYDIA
". . . a sea-change/into something rich and strange."
Wm. Shakespeare

Just now, I wish for someone
like me, but newer, for whom this
pebbled beach will be rinsed back suddenly
into something pure, for whom
these breakers will flatten themselves,
obeisant, at your feet, wetting
each stone into its particular
self.

Just now, as we walk the edge,
I want for you the companion eye,
a hand like mine (but younger) reaching
for moonstones, agates, trans-
lucencies in apricot, onyx, amber,
milk-white, each water-true. Your glance
singles out a winking bead of aqua
sea-glass. Call it a mermaid's
tear. Call it an eye; it looks
back.

And when, from the cold
lip of a wave, your fingers rescue
a marble of quartzite from a million
others, and place its desire in my palm,
just now I witness a wish turning
true.

MOBILE

Freed by a nomad wind,
all afternoon the aspen leaves,
like grown children,
leave home. The color of

moonrise, they drift
and eddy on the twilight
mirrors, on those eyes of light
where the stream pools

at the end of a dry season.
Changelings, the yellow hearts
swim on the brim
between world and stars

in a brief, giddy autonomy.
Tonight the first
frost will lock around them
its slow fingers.

FAILED BLIZZARD

All day the sky threatened, like lead—
its weight, and the same color. "The big
one," everyone prognosticated. The air
hung on our restlessness, snow
waiting to fall, wind holding its
breath, thermometer stuck below zero.
How we wanted the blizzard—craving
our own heroism, reading the snow plow,
logs piled, kettles of pea soup simmering
for stranded travellers.
We invoked the hiss of snow on
the window glass, the scream of wind
carving the drifts at the house corners,
all night the groan of the house at
its joints. We yearned to see
the whole world leveled white,
ourselves trapped around the glowing
woodstove with mugs of chocolate,
cracking intrepid winter jokes,
and after a couple of days stormbound
making it into town, nearly frozen, by ski.
Already we could see our t-shirts:
"I survived the blizzard of '94."

By late afternoon we were getting bored
with the weather channel; the front

faltered, broke, bits of it drifting
south. The anticlimax felt
like a lover's failure to come.
For days we were eating pea soup.

THE TODAY SHOW

It starts with the thin black line
visible from the front window, an isobar
across our sky. On the morning
forecast, the weather man, expansive as
the rising sun, blocking the western states

with his body, has us down for the 50s
and our state colored lime (sherbet, between
lemon and raspberry). Outside,
sure enough the fields, even the roofs,
are brushed with a radiant dayglo.

Committing our day to partly sunny,
the map exhibits a scatter of emblems:
clouds hover, suns grinning around
their left edges; knives of lightning
dart over Omaha; stars dust the Rockies

with snow; fronts overtake us with their
red promises, blue threats. The jet stream
curves over Oregon, sinister, a worm
in space, pulsing. A low is driving in
from the Pacific and already my mind wears

the film of white, a glove clotted
with snow. Somewhere the satellite hums.
In a dot of a city the meteorologists do their
supple graphics on a screen, and the whole
continent lights up like a neon sign to God.

M. C. ESCHER'S THREE WORLDS

FOR JOHN SHAW

The leaves — we recognize beech, birch, oak, maple —
    all dead,
float thinly on the silver cheek of the lake, film its
alien skin with pale freckles, mark a glass floor,

a boundary stilled in time by a dead artist.
    Underneath —
like a porcelain inlay — the round-eyed carp has
lurked for decades in the water's dark enamel

which, by some magic, is lucid enough to accept
    light and
hold it on paper. Rooting in the water mirror, the bare
branches are only abstractions of themselves

at two removes, recognizable but reversed, a
    platonic idea
of trees. The top rim of this rendering we discern
as the bottom of the real, guessing that for Escher

actual elms stretched up from there, on an edge
    of land
fictional for us except as probability. Really,
the fish, tensed like a question mark, in ambush

behind the scrim of leaves and shadow-branches, is
    the only
live thing in these monochrome worlds. And even it

waits motionless within the print, like some
curious paperweight object suspended in acrylic,
     preserved
in its long, upward observation of our otherness, as if
inquiring: Do you, too, define yourselves as part

of some creator's dream? Are you veiled in
     questions,
leaf-lapped, tangled in an eternal twilight by
intimations of celestial trees?

EATING THE WHOLE EGG

FOR MY GREAT-GRANDFATHER

Oral history tells us you went through
three wives. One story is that
every day you breakfasted with
your current spouse on toast
and a three-minute egg,
chipping off its white cap in the precise
British way, and in a grand gesture,
spooning to your wife that minor albumen,
watery, pale as her self. That was her meal;
you feasted on yolk, rich and yellow
as a gold sovereign, and crushed the shells,
feeding them by gritty doses to
your offspring lined up along the table—
a supplement to stave off rickets and
accustom the family to patriarchy.

Nourished thus on remnants and rigor,
your tribe multiplied to twenty-two.
The legend astonishes me still. And I
still bear, along with traces of those women's
genes, a vestigial guilt
whenever I cook myself a breakfast egg
and then devour it, white, yolk,
protein, cholesterol, and all. Like
seeing the sun after generations of moons.
Like being the golden egg and eating it too.

THE LIBRARIAN

For centuries now the old-growth forest,
a victim, but also a devourer of the world,
has pulled into its slow boil of seasons,
into its emerald mouth behind the hills, the sky's
gold light, the elements of air, the holy fluids—
creeks, rains, winter fogs—trapping clouds
of flying seeds, requiring the death of leaves
for a humus rich and dark as old leather,
rotting in small clumps the intricate bones of birds,
translating all this fleshy language,
holding its secret meanings like words
in a net of vines and roots. The forest writes its
diligent renewal in flourishes of green ink.

This wilderness—who's to read it?—
this volume buried in a forgotten archive,
waiting for some scholar like you—hunter
of all the lore hidden in its rare
forest folio, luxuriant as my self, a book
of mysteries. Whose pages you have parted,
      reading
between my lines, eyes and fingers darting
like foxes. I am a jungle penetrated, a rough draft
of woman, my thickets drenched with the rain
of your man tears, my unlit rivers swimming
with your seed. Beneath the planets of your eyes
my mountains rise. Your mouth is mine;
with every fertile word you wake me green.

ORIENTING

This night is multi-leveled.
By that I mean I am sliced
in layers, walking the beach path
at eleven p.m. Scattered high —
broken glass on an infinite
parking lot — the stars seem
sharp enough to scratch my eyes.
Lower down the tops of trees,
dark and undifferentiated,
boil like a line of low clouds.
And there between the trees
the horizon glitters, a silver lip
between earth and heaven.

Around me at chest level fog settles
in strips thick as bandages,
drifting between me and my feet
so that every step I take
hides from me. I am divided, myself
from myself, like one of Escher's
spiral people unfurling in
a ribbon. I peer through aqueous air,
shivering with paradox: seeing so far,
hesitating so near.

But this is a universe that grinds
at glib appearances. Gravity
pulls at me relentlessly

through my soles. Infinity beckons.
And when a wedge of air, silent
as Spirit, like a knife from the Sound,
cuts across the marshes, it peels back
the cataract of fog almost surgically.
Gauze rolls off in layers until
I am joined again, moving ahead, foot
by foot, steering both by the stars
and the stones on the path.

Written at Orient, Long Island, August 1990

MORE AND MORE ...

... I find myself coinciding
with myself. I meet me coming
and going and when I think of me,
there I am, quite often. I'm getting hard
to escape; I used to be hard to find.

What irony, when I have been everywhere,
my life spread so wide—flung, taut, like a single
bedsheet stretched to cover the whole world.
Thinned to transparency, a bubble bursting.
Stalled, a wave too spent to conquer the beach.

Now, though, it's like double vision—when
your eyes finally get it right, and pull
the split image into one. I see myself mirrored,
clean at all my edges, even the hairs around my head
in focus, the sun blazing them into a halo.

GOLDEN DELICIOUS

Last night's killing frost uncolored
the whole of the Skagit. This afternoon,
hiking the valley, I found
a spread of apple trees gone wild—
black nets of branches
heavy with yellow fruit, frozen
solid enough to last the winter.

If the freeze had held them
in its hand, vise-hard, not let go . . .

But a rogue river of wind, come loose
from the Sound at noon, began
to thaw the valley rotten.
Now the numbed apples are falling,
one, one, one, till the gray ground boils
with bruised gold, hanging the old orchard's
autumn air with the winy smell of loss.

I BEGIN TO UNDERSTAND
HOW WEATHER

The wet gusts that all Friday afternoon
swept the mountains with their gray silk
skirts — their cold cloth rinsed my face —

have calmed and re-combined tonight
in this placid black backwater under
my cabin window. They show their stormy origins —

ripples fretted like clouds, and liquid
light dodging an awkward moon that stares,
double-faced, from sky, from water. I begin

to understand how weather, like verse, like
music, plays with pieces of the past, makes
new of old, turns up the ribbed silver on the under-

side of the leaf. From God knows where,
miracles come. And for you I am making this
small, fresh blessing from fallen rain.

BEACH, ABERYSTWYTH

Without expecting anything profound we were,
    as always, magnetized
by the idea of sea, drawn down the stone steps
    to the shingle,
with the blue-black sky glooming behind light-washed
    pastel verticals
on our left—the beach hotels. We turned away from
    the morning glare,
crunched along the shoal into the stretched shadow of
    the broken castle,
dodged the scatter of debris left by the Bank Holiday
    crowds. Then,
as if our ears suddenly came open, the sea's huge
    sound hit—waves
pounding forward into thunder, then sucking back
    and away

through what sounded like skeletons—a bruising
    grind and rattle,
racket and clutch as though a cobble of vertebrae had
    been thrown up
to sieve the Irish Sea. This boneyard hummed up
    through our soles. Our ears
rang with the songs of fierce minimal stones. Mussel
    shells lay about,
sprung open like pill boxes, stinging the view (such
    livid blue
inside the dull black casings). And the small surprises

of sea-glass,
eyes clipped from once-useful green and cobalt
    bottles, the colors
of oceans condensed, rubbed by a marine restlessness
    to fragments

soft and blind as sea breath. Crab carapaces gone
    limp, no longer
crisp with life. The sea itself sliced by knives of wind,
    latticed
like fish scales, hiding beneath its netted frown
    a glimmer of pearls
and shells, and jellies floating deep like perfect,
    archetypal
parachutes of light—invisible, but we knew they were
    there. And we.
Since Eden we have been wanderers, blasted with
    wind-driven sand,
sometimes scattered wide like driftwood, like the great
    leg bones
of sea monsters, sometimes a mere flash of rinded
    color left

on the shore with the stranded rose red kelp bladders,
    the plastic
cups, the soaked beach rags of the careless. We need
    reminding
of what we were meant to be before we reached too
    far, too fast,
and were forced to feel the chop of the fire blade, the
    despairing bubble

of flood, the wrack, the ruin. This is what we have
    become: flesh, splendid,
weak, and brief; only our bones and souls persist.
    Just before noon
the moment's fair weather drained away like a spirit
    rising, the light wiped
from the faces of the hotels, the dark castle crumbling,
    grain by grain.

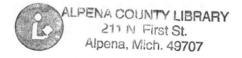

MAKING A PATH:
TUOLUMNE MEADOWS

Take the first step towards where
you want to go, then keep going, brushing
through the manzanitas, crushing the sweet grass
of the valley floor so its pungency
seasons the air, flowing lively as the trout stream
at your right hand, all color and gleam.
On meadow grass you are sketching a new course
that will echo the current, will skip and dodge in

and out of willow shadows on the bank
of its ancient water-path for fish. You
are no fly fisherman, but after you
the quiet carriers of rod and creel
will follow, several in a month,
and, almost without thinking, obey your
rabbit track, verifying the subtle hollow
being carved between tufts of brittle sedge,

a coarse growth, bleached as the hair
of your children's heads in August, years ago.
Your walking has woven, unhurried
as a Kashmiri rug, a narrow runner of turf
with threads of tan, greens fading,
burnt ambers, straw. Will the winter snow
bleach out the subtleties, and iron
the field fabric flat? Does all this have to

start over every spring? How many footfalls
go to make a meadow path? Buechner said beat
a trail to God long enough, he will come to you
on the trail you have beaten, bringing you the gift
of himself. Abruptly, evening shadows the meadow,
but you keep pacing along and along
your own slow track. In whose fisherman boots
will you meet him, coming the other way?

WRITING THE RIVER

After two day's rain heavy enough to
circle the view with descending silver
Beaver Creek has grown to the size of

a metaphor—rising fast from summer,
slow over pebbles, to this rowdy
torrent. Under my window it hurls itself,

with the force of myth, over river stones,
down rapids, riddled with fish.
All day the voice of water roars

behind my writing—all day, while I'm
making soup, stoking the woodstove
(the flames rushing their orange rivers

up the chimney). Under a darkening sky
I step out on the porch to check its
scouring race, and is it rising still? It is

myself I am checking, keeping the window
open all night to that naked
splendid sound, dark as pewter. Rainfall

and river together—rinsing the room,
soaking my dreams. In one dream
I am a salmon working my way up

the valley, grazed by rocks. I am living
a creek, writing a river. Downstream,
a trace of my blood feeds the Sound.

AUTHOR

LUCI SHAW was born in England in 1928, and grew up in Australia and Canada before coming to the U.S. to attend college and marry. She is author of six books of poems, among them *Listen to the Green*, *Postcard From the Shore*, and *Polishing the Petoskey Stone* as well as an autobiographical prose work *God in the Dark: Through Grief and Beyond*. She has also edited three poetry anthologies. Shaw is writer in residence at Regent College, Vancouver, Canada, and an adjunct faculty member of New College, Berkeley. She lives in California with her husband, John Hoyte.